EARLY PEOPLES

ANCIENT EGYPTIANS

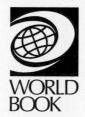

WORLD
BOOK

World Book
a Scott Fetzer company
Chicago
www.worldbookonline.com

World Book, Inc.
233 N. Michigan Avenue
Chicago, IL 60601
U.S.A.

For information about other World Book publications, visit our Web site at http://www.worldbookonline.com or call 1-800-WORLDBK (967-5325).
For information about sales to schools and libraries, call 1-800-975-3250 (United States), or 1-800-837-5365 (Canada).

Library of Congress Cataloging-in-Publication Data

Ancient Egyptians.
    p. cm. -- (Early peoples)
  Includes index.
    Summary: "A discussion of the early Egyptians, including who the people were, where they lived, the rise of civilization, social structure, religion, art and architecture, science and technology, daily life, entertainment and sports. Features include timelines, fact boxes, glossary, list of recommended reading and web sites, and index"-- Provided by publisher.
    ISBN 978-0-7166-2129-4
    1. Egypt--Civilization--To 332 B.C.--Juvenile literature. 2. Egypt--Social life and customs--To 332 B.C.--Juvenile literature. I. World Book, Inc.
  DT61.A626 2009
  932--dc22
                                        2008039953

Printed in China by Leo Paper Products Ltd., Heshan, Guangdong
2nd printing June 2010

STAFF

EXECUTIVE COMMITTEE
President
  Paul A. Gazzolo
Vice President and Chief Marketing Officer
  Patricia Ginnis
Vice President and Chief Financial Officer
  Donald D. Keller
Vice President and Editor in Chief
  Paul A. Kobasa
Director, Human Resources
  Bev Ecker
Chief Technology Officer
  Tim Hardy
Managing Director, International
  Benjamin Hinton

EDITORIAL
Editor in Chief
  Paul A. Kobasa
Associate Director, Supplementary Publications
  Scott Thomas
Managing Editor, Supplementary Publications
  Barbara A. Mayes
Senior Editor, Supplementary Publications
  Kristina Vaicikonis
Manager, Research, Supplementary Publications
  Cheryl Graham
Manager, Contracts & Compliance
  (Rights & Permissions)
  Loranne K. Shields

Administrative Assistant
  Ethel Matthews
Editors
  Nicholas Kilzer
  Scott Richardson
  Christine Sullivan

GRAPHICS AND DESIGN
Associate Director
  Sandra M. Dyrlund
Manager,
  Tom Evans
Coordinator, Design Development and Production
  Brenda B. Tropinski

EDITORIAL ADMINISTRATION
Director, Systems and Projects
  Tony Tills
Senior Manager, Publishing Operations
  Timothy Falk

PRODUCTION
Director, Manufacturing and Pre-Press
  Carma Fazio
Manufacturing Manager
  Steve Hueppchen
Production/Technology Manager
  Anne Fritzinger
Production Specialist
  Curley Hunter
Proofreader
  Emilie Schrage

MARKETING
Chief Marketing Officer
  Patricia Ginnis
Associate Director, School and Library Marketing
  Jennifer Parello

Produced for World Book by
  White-Thomson Publishing Ltd.
  0044 (0)845 362 8240
  www.wtpub.co.uk
  Steve White-Thomson, President

Writer: Andrew Langley
Editor: Kelly Davis
Designer: Clare Nicholas
Photo Researcher: Amy Sparks
Map Artist: Stefan Chabluk
Illustrator: Adam Hook (p. 25)
Fact Checker: Chelsey Hankins
Proofreader: Catherine Gardner
Indexer: Nila Glikin

Consultant: Dr. Kathryn E. Piquette
Institute of Archaeology
University College London
United Kingdom

TABLE OF CONTENTS

Glossary There is a glossary on pages 60-61. Terms defined in the glossary are in type **that looks like this** on their first appearance on any spread (two facing pages).

Additional Resources Books for further reading and recommended Web sites are listed on page 62. Because of the nature of the Internet, some Web site addresses may have changed since publication. The publisher has no responsibility for any such changes or for the content of cited sources.

WHO WERE THE ANCIENT EGYPTIANS?

The ancient Egyptians were a people who created one of the world's first great **civilizations**. It developed about 5,000 years ago in the valley of the Nile River, in northeastern Africa. The **culture** lasted for more than 3,000 years.

Ancient Egypt consisted of a long narrow strip of **fertile** land with desert on each side. The mighty Nile flowed through the middle of this fertile strip, bringing a regular supply of water. Every year, the river flooded, covering the **flood plain** with fertile soil. This allowed Egyptian farmers to raise large amounts of crops to feed the people.

THE GREAT PYRAMID

The Great Pyramid at Giza (above, center) is the largest of all the Egyptian pyramids. It was originally 481 feet (147 meters) high, but because of erosion it stands about 450 feet (137 meters) high today. The pyramid contains more than 2 million blocks of stone, some of them weighing as much as 15 tons (13.6 metric tons). The Great Pyramid was built with astonishing accuracy. Its base is almost exactly level, and the four sides are nearly the same length from the base to the top. Of the Seven Wonders of the Ancient World, the Great Pyramid of Giza is the only one still standing.

What Did the Ancient Egyptians Achieve?

The Egyptians conquered large areas of nearby lands. By 3100 B.C., they ruled a region that stretched for over 1,000 miles (1,600 kilometers), from the Mediterranean Sea in the north to present-day Sudan in the south. The Egyptians also built up trading links with other parts of North Africa and southwest Asia.

The ancient Egyptians built great cities, such as Thebes *(theebz)*. They developed one of the first national governments. Ancient Egypt was ruled by a king, known in later times as the pharaoh *(FAIR oh)*. The Egyptians created their own calendar, a kind of paper called **papyrus** *(puh PY ruhs)*, and **hieroglyphics** *(HY uhr uh GLIHF ihkz)*, a form of writing using pictures. The ancient Egyptians believed in life after death, and their religion was complex, with many gods and **rituals**.

Temples and Pyramids

The ancient Egyptians are known for their buildings. The **pyramids** at Giza *(GEE zuh)* are some of the most amazing structures ever created. They were built as tombs, where Egyptian kings were buried along with some of their queens and other family members. The pyramids have survived for thousands of years, along with other famous works such as the **Sphinx** *(sfihngks)*—a huge stone figure with a human head and a lion's body—and the Temple of Karnak, ancient Egypt's largest temple.

▼ Farmers in modern Egypt still raise crops using techniques from ancient times. They take water from the Nile River using such ancient devices as the shadoof *(shah DOOF)*, shown in the foreground below. A shadoof is a long rod with a bucket on one end and a weight on the other, used to raise water from a river. The water then flows along a channel to the fields.

WHERE DID THE ANCIENT EGYPTIANS LIVE?

▲ Beyond the green and fertile land at the edge of the Nile lie low desert, barren rock cliffs, and the high desert.

Ancient Egypt lay along the valley of the Nile River. This great river, the longest in the world, flows for 4,160 miles (6,695 kilometers) through northeast Africa. The Nile begins near the equator and flows northward, through northeast Africa, into the Mediterranean Sea. Near the Mediterranean coast, the river fans out into many channels, forming the Nile **Delta**. The river flowed through ancient Egypt for over 600 miles (nearly 1,000 kilometers).

The land alongside the river is lush and green with plants, thanks to the supply of water. In ancient times, the Nile Valley was also rich in birds, animals, and fish. Beyond this green strip, however, lies a vast desert, where there is little rain and few plants grow. The Egyptians called this place Deshret (*deh SHRET*), meaning "Red Land."

The Nile Flood

Before dams were built on the Nile in modern times, the river flooded the valley every summer. Heavy rains in the far south drain into the river. This causes the level of the Nile to rise downstream beyond Egypt. Before dams were built, the Nile would flood over its banks by July, covering the land on either side. In September, the waters went down again.

The floodwaters left behind a layer of rich black **silt**, carried down from the highlands. The silt created a **fertile** strip of land, which averaged about 6 miles (10 kilometers) in width on each side of the river. Crops grew well here, especially in the sun of the following winter and spring.

THE NILE CATARACTS

On most of its way north, the Nile flows smoothly and slowly. But in several places it passes over stretches of rock. Here the water is much shallower and it runs quickly around many boulders and small islands. These stretches of rocky rapids are called **cataracts** (*KAT uh rakts*). There are six main Nile cataracts. The first (farthest north) is at Aswan (*AS wahn*) in present-day Egypt. In ancient times, this was as far as boats could travel upstream, unless they were portaged (carried overland), or canals were dug to bypass the cataract. The photograph below, taken in the late 1860's, shows the first cataract on the Nile River.

THE ORIGINS OF THE ANCIENT EGYPTIANS AND THEIR EARLY HISTORY

Humans came to the area now known as Egypt more than 9,000 years ago. They were nomadic people, moving from place to place in search of food. They would have hunted for game and gathered other food in the lush grasslands.

The Early Egyptians

Over time, the climate of the region became hotter and drier. The whole region gradually turned to desert, except for the Nile Valley. People were forced to move to the **fertile** strip along the river. Here, about 9,000 years ago, they built the first settlements and learned to grow crops.

The early settlements in ancient Egypt grew into villages and towns. Communities formed in different areas. As these groups became bigger, they joined together or conquered one another.

By about 3100 B.C., ancient Egypt was made up of two kingdoms. In the north, Lower Egypt included the people around the Nile **Delta.** In the south, Upper Egypt stretched to the First **Cataract** in the Nile. According to **legend**, the king of Upper Egypt at this time was called Menes (*MEE neez*). Some historians think that Menes may have been the

▼ The Narmer Palette celebrated the victory of King Narmer over his enemies. (Narmer has been identified by some scholars as the same person as King Menes.) This large stone palette was likely a temple gift.

THE DYNASTIES OF ANCIENT EGYPT

According to legend, Menes was the first king of Egypt, and he established what later historians call the first **dynasty** (*DY nuh stee*), or series of rulers that were often from the same family. There would be about 30 dynasties over the next 3,000 years of history in ancient Egypt. During this period, more than 150 kings and queens ruled. Historians have given each dynasty a number in Roman numerals, to make it easier to understand the long history of ancient Egypt.

same person as an actual king called Narmer *(NAHR muhr)*. Narmer gained control over Lower Egypt and united the two regions into one country. With this, the **civilization** of ancient Egypt began.

The Old Kingdom—the Age of the Pyramids

The first great period of ancient Egyptian history is called the Old Kingdom. This time period lasted from about 2650 B.C. until about 2150 B.C. During this time, Egypt established a strong central government headed by the king. The early rulers founded the city of Memphis *(mehm fus)*, which lay on the border between Upper and Lower Egypt.

Most of the great **pyramids** of ancient Egypt were built during the Old Kingdom. These huge structures were built as royal tombs. They also had associated temples for the **cults** *(kuhltz)* of kings and queens, who were believed to be gods. The first known pyramid was the Step Pyramid at Saqqarah *(sahk KAH rah)*, dating to about 2650 B.C.

The Old Kingdom ended in civil war and violence. There was a long period of **drought** *(drowt)*, when the Nile failed to rise high enough to flood the lands. Crops did not grow, and many people starved. The royal family began to lose control, and many **nomarchs** *(NOM ahrkz)*, or local governors, rebelled against them. Mobs attacked tombs and palaces. Soon, invaders moved in from Nubia *(NOO bee uh)*, which was to the south of Egypt.

▶ An **ivory** carving of a king wearing the crown of Upper Egypt. Found in Abydos, the statue dates from around 3000 B.C.

THE MIDDLE KINGDOM—FROM AROUND 1975 B.C. TO 1640 B.C.

Between the end of the Old Kingdom and the start of the Middle Kingdom was the First Intermediate Period. During this time, the lands of ancient Egypt were not united under one king. Local rulers—**nomarchs**—became the most important rulers. Eventually, these local rulers began to fight for power. Two sites—Herakleopolis Magna *(hehr AKH lee YOH poh lihs MAG nuh)* in the north and Thebes in the south—became the main centers of power.

In about 1975 B.C., in the later part of **Dynasty XI**, Egypt was united again under the ruler Mentuhotep *(mehn TOO hoh tehp)*. In Dynasty XII, a series of strong rulers seized power. The first of them was Amenemhet *(ah MEHN ehm heht)* I, who established a new capital city near Memphis. The reunification of Egypt as a single kingdom marked the start of the second great period of ancient Egyptian history, known as the Middle Kingdom.

Taking Control

The rulers of Dynasty XII made Egypt's defenses stronger. King Senusret III *(she NOOS reht)* built a string of mud-brick forts along the southern part of the Nile to keep out the Nubians and control trade.

The new rulers imposed their control on the nomarchs who had grown so powerful. While the nomarchs had once been appointed by the king, during the interim period the position of nomarch had become **hereditary** *(huh REHD uh tehr ee)*. Nomarchs began to build their own tombs and appointed their own priests to look after their **cults.** The nomarchs had essentially

▲ A painted, carved **stele** *(STEE lee)*—an upright stone slab with writing—shows a Middle Kingdom official and his wife. The stele, found at Abydos, dates from 1938–1755 B.C.

become kings over their regions. Under the changes of the Middle Kingdom, the nomarchs were forced to pay heavy taxes and provide troops for the Egyptian army. The kings of the Middle Kingdom closed the nomarchs' **courts** and took away many of their privileges. The position lost its hereditary status, and local rulers were again appointed by, and more loyal to, the king.

Prosperity and Decline

Rulers of the Middle Kingdom made Egypt wealthy again. They conquered Nubia and reopened trade links with Palestine and Syria. King Amenemhet III drained marshes in the Fayyum *(fah YOOM)* region to create new land for farming. Other kings enlarged the great temple to the god Amun *(AH muhn)* at Karnak.

In about 1756 B.C., Dynasty XII gave way to Dynasties XIII and XIV. Once again, the Egyptian kings began to lose control of their land. Settlers from southwest Asia—perhaps from the area that is present-day Israel, Palestine, and Lebanon—had been moving into the **Delta** region throughout the Middle Kingdom. These people, whom the Egyptians called the Hyksos *(HIHK sohs)*, brought with them chariots and other new weapons and technology. By about 1630 B.C., the Hyksos had seized power, and the Middle Kingdom came to an end.

▶ A map showing the extent of lands held by Egypt during the Old, Middle, and New kingdoms.

ANCIENT NUBIA

Nubia was a region of ancient Africa that covered the southernmost part of present-day Egypt and most of present-day Sudan. Although Nubia was often controlled by ancient Egypt, powerful states independent of Egypt sometimes arose there, and Nubians maintained their own **cultures**, worshiped their own gods, and had their own forms of architecture.

Old Kingdom (about 2650 to 2150 B.C.)
Middle Kingdom (about 1975 to 1640 B.C.)
New Kingdom (about 1539 to 1075 B.C.)

THE NEW KINGDOM—FROM AROUND 1539 B.C. TO 1075 B.C.

The period from around 1640 B.C. to around 1539 B.C. is known as the Second Intermediate Period. During this period, the Hyksos ruled the northern part of the Nile valley.

In about 1600 B.C., the kings of Upper Egypt began a war of liberation against the Hyksos. After a long struggle, they drove the Hyksos out of the country. The leader of the kings of Upper Egypt, Ahmose *(AH mohs)* I, became the first king of **Dynasty** XVIII in about 1539 B.C. This was the beginning of ancient Egypt's third and greatest period, which historians now call the New Kingdom. It lasted for about 500 years. During this period, Egypt grew into one of the ancient world's strongest powers.

The Egyptian Empire

The rulers of this new dynasty built up a permanent army, using chariots and other military equipment adopted from the Hyksos. The Egyptians conquered the areas that would become known as Palestine and Syria, extending the frontiers of Egypt to the Orontes *(oh RUHN tees)* River in the northeast. In the south, Nubia became an Egyptian province. Riches from these lands poured into Egypt and were used to decorate magnificent new temples, tombs, and palaces.

Akhenaten and the New God

For many centuries, most Egyptians had worshiped Amun as the most important of the gods. But in 1353 B.C., Amenhotep *(ah MEHN hoh tehp)* IV came to the throne and made a dramatic change to Egyptian religion. The new king declared there was only one god—not Amun but an aspect of the sun god called Aten *(AH tuhn)*.

Amenhotep even changed his own name to Akhenaten *(ah kuh NAH tehn)*, which means "He who serves or is beneficial to the Aten." Akhenaten also built a new capital city at Amarna *(uh MAR nuh)*, which he called Akhetaten *(ah kuh TAH tehn)*, meaning "Horizon of Aten."

◀ A huge statue of Ramses II, with a princess, perhaps one of his daughters, standing between his feet. Ramses II ruled Egypt from about 1279 to 1213 B.C.

Akhenaten closed down many of Amun's temples and ordered that the old god's name be removed from monuments. After Akhenaten's death, his successors ended the religious changes and returned to the traditional **cult** of the god Amun.

Among the pharaohs to follow after Akhenaten were two great military leaders, Seti *(SEH tee)* I and his son Ramses *(RAM seez)* II. They defeated the Hittites *(HIH tyts)*, a rising power in the Middle East, and strengthened Egyptian control of Nubia.

▼ The tomb of Hatshepsut *(hat SHEHP soot)*, in the Valley of the Kings, is considered one of the great artistic achievements of the New Kingdom. Hatshepsut was a woman pharaoh who ruled in her own right. In statues and paintings, she is often depicted wearing the clothing of a male pharaoh and a ceremonial beard.

TIMELINE OF ANCIENT EGYPTIAN HISTORY
Approximate Dates

3100 B.C.–2686 B.C. King Narmer (possibly the same person as the legendary King Menes) unites Upper and Lower Egypt; The Early Dynastic Period: Dynasties I through II

2650 B.C.–2150 B.C. The Old Kingdom: Dynasties III through VI; the building of the Great **Pyramid**

2150 B.C.–1975 B.C. First Intermediate Period: Dynasties IX through XI

1975 B.C.–1640 B.C. The Middle Kingdom: Dynasties XI through XIV

1640 B.C.–1539 B.C. Second Intermediate Period: Dynasties XV through XVII; rule of northern Egypt by the Hyksos

1539 B.C.–1075 B.C. The New Kingdom: Dynasties XVIII through XX

THE RULERS

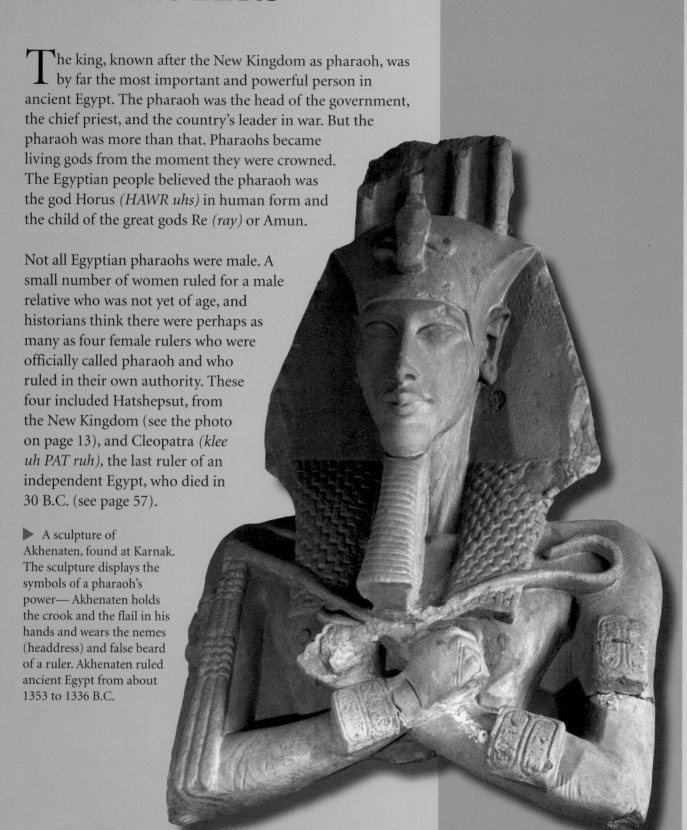

The king, known after the New Kingdom as pharaoh, was by far the most important and powerful person in ancient Egypt. The pharaoh was the head of the government, the chief priest, and the country's leader in war. But the pharaoh was more than that. Pharaohs became living gods from the moment they were crowned. The Egyptian people believed the pharaoh was the god Horus *(HAWR uhs)* in human form and the child of the great gods Re *(ray)* or Amun.

Not all Egyptian pharaohs were male. A small number of women ruled for a male relative who was not yet of age, and historians think there were perhaps as many as four female rulers who were officially called pharaoh and who ruled in their own authority. These four included Hatshepsut, from the New Kingdom (see the photo on page 13), and Cleopatra *(klee uh PAT ruh)*, the last ruler of an independent Egypt, who died in 30 B.C. (see page 57).

▶ A sculpture of Akhenaten, found at Karnak. The sculpture displays the symbols of a pharaoh's power— Akhenaten holds the crook and the flail in his hands and wears the nemes (headdress) and false beard of a ruler. Akhenaten ruled ancient Egypt from about 1353 to 1336 B.C.

Symbols of Power

From the Old Kingdom period, male rulers sometimes wore a special costume on ceremonial occasions, which showed their importance. Instead of the common loincloth, the pharaoh wore a pleated skirt, or kilt *(kihlt)*. From the back of his belt hung a bull's tail, which was probably a sign that he had the power of a bull. He carried two signs of his kingship—a crook (a stick used by shepherds) and an object shaped like a **flail** *(flayl),* a tool used for separating grain or seeds from the rest of the plant.

On his head the pharaoh often wore a striped cloth called a **nemes** *(neh meez),* which hung down on both sides of the face and was gathered in the back. Attached to the front of this headdress was an ornament in the shape of a rearing cobra, the form of one of the gods believed to protect the king. The ruler also wore a false beard.

DEATH OF A PHARAOH

The death of a pharaoh was a crucial moment in Egyptian society. A new king had to be crowned, and the old king was ushered into the afterlife with the proper **rituals**. The **mortuary temple** became a center of worship dedicated to the king's memory. In this way, the old king would live on as a god and continue to protect Egypt.

After **mummification**, priests wrapped the king's body in cloth. It was taken by funeral barge across the river to the site of the royal tomb. In Old Kingdom times this might have been a **pyramid.** From the New Kingdom onward, most pharaohs chose to be buried in tombs carved into the cliffs of the remote Valley of the Kings near Thebes.

▲ A painted limestone carving of Nefertiti *(NEHF uhr TEE tee)*, a wife of Akhenaten. The bust was made by a famous sculptor Thutmose *(thoot MOH suh),* and it was found in his workshop. Art made during the time of the reign of Akhenaten is in the Amarna style, which features elongated (lengthened) features. This lengthening can be seen in both Nefertiti's neck and Akhenaten's face.

THE STATE OFFICIALS

The pharaoh was supreme ruler of ancient Egypt, but officials oversaw most of the daily running of the government. A large number of ministers and other officials surrounded the pharaoh. In the early periods, the king chose these people from his own royal family.

By the Middle Kingdom, however, an entire class of officials had formed. Sons inherited government positions from their fathers, and daughters served as musicians and priestesses in the temples. These families grew wealthy and powerful. They lived in grand houses and built elaborate tombs that had at one time only been allowed for the royal family.

▼ An inner chamber in the tomb of a vizier who served an Old Kingdom ruler in Egypt. The walls are decorated with carvings of servants.

The Viziers

The most important of the government officials were the **viziers** *(vih ZIHRZ)*. There was one vizier for all of Egypt during the Old and Middle Kingdom periods. Two viziers served Egypt at the start of the New Kingdom—one vizier served Upper Egypt and one Lower Egypt.

The main work of a vizier was to make daily reports to the pharaoh, to issue instructions to the various government departments, and to appoint (or dismiss) other officials. For this, the vizier had a large work-force of **scribes**, guards, and other servants.

The vizier had other important jobs. As the chief tax official, he made sure that taxes were collected throughout Egypt. The vizier was also the chief justice. In the palace law court, he made judgments in important criminal cases.

Treasurers and Nomarchs

There were many other high officials. The taxes and other payments were stored in the temples and the king's storehouses. Most of the payments were in the form of crops and other products. The overseer *(OH vuhr see uhr)* of the treasury kept control of these vast stores of wealth.

Egypt was divided into 42 provinces called **nomes** *(nohmz).* These provinces were ruled by **nomarchs.** During the period of the Old Kingdom, the nomarchs were **hereditary** positions. By the start of the Middle Kingdom period, the pharaoh began to appoint a nomarch to govern each province. Even with this change, these local governors still held great power within their own region—they were in control of everything within their nome, from tax-collection to overseeing the temples. This power sometimes tempted them to rebel against the central government of the pharaoh.

▶ A stone statue of a vizier sitting cross-legged with a **papyrus** document unrolled on his knees.

PRIESTS AND PRIESTESSES

There were many different kinds of temples throughout ancient Egypt. Most of these sacred sites were looked after by priests and priestesses.

Being a priest or priestess was an important job. When they performed their priestly work at a temple, they were representing the king. Despite the importance of the job, however, a person of the priestly class lived modestly. He or she bathed twice a day to stay clean and pure. In the New Kingdom period, some priests shaved their entire bodies regularly in order to be thought pure. They normally wore simple white linen clothing and sandals made from **papyrus**. A priest was not permitted to wear any item made from an animal, such as leather garments or sandals.

Temple Work

Every important god or goddess in ancient Egypt had his or her own temple. Depending on the god's importance, this might be a small mud-brick building or a huge stone complex with courtyards, halls, and storage areas.

The forecourt (outer court) of a temple was open to everyone, but only a king or priest could enter the temple rooms or the inner **sanctuary** *(SANGK chu EHR ee)*. This inner area was where the statue of the god was kept.

PROFESSIONAL PRIESTS

Not until the New Kingdom did priests become a separate class in ancient Egypt. Before that time, men served as priests for a certain period of time and then went back to doing their usual jobs, perhaps as doctors or **scribes**. These priests might serve for a month and then have a three-month break before having to serve again. Even after a class of professional priests arose, part-time priests were still used in smaller temples.

◄ A sistrum *(SIHS truhm)* of **bronze** and gold, dating from around 1000 B.C., was used in the worship of Amun. Similar to a rattle, sistrums would have been played by temple musicians.

Working in the Temple

Religious ceremonies took place every day in the temples across the land. Egyptians believed these **rituals** were vital to keeping peace and order in the world. They believed that the gods would look after the Egyptian people, providing the gods were properly worshiped and "fed." This was the job of men and women who served as priests and priestesses.

The Daily Ritual

Every morning, a temple priest entered the sanctuary and opened the door of the box shrine, which contained a statue of the god or goddess to which that temple was devoted. The priest greeted the statue with prayers, removed it from the shrine, and washed and clothed it. He then laid out offerings of food and wine and walked backwards out of the sanctuary, so as not to turn away from the statue. He brushed away his footprints as he left. Later, he returned to remove the offerings. This routine was repeated later at midday and evening meal times. At the end of the day, the priest put the statue back into the shrine for the night.

▶ A red granite statue that dates to about 2650 B.C. The statue depicts an ancient Egyptian priest wearing a wig and a short kilt.

SOLDIERS AND WARFARE

▲ A scene from a painted wooden chest found in the tomb of Tutankhamun *(toot ahngk AH muhn)* shows the pharaoh driving a chariot into battle.

During the Old Kingdom and Middle Kingdom periods, Egypt had no standing army. When the king needed soldiers to defend the borders or escort groups of traders, he would ask local governors to gather troops. These were fairly untrained infantrymen (foot soldiers), often armed with spears, shields, and bows.

The rise of the Hyksos at the end of the Middle Kingdom caused the Egyptians to realize the importance of trained troops and new weapons. The pharaohs built up a much bigger, permanent army. They adopted many of the weapons of the Hyksos' soldiers, including stronger bows and horse-drawn chariots.

The Life of a Soldier

A soldier's life in ancient Egypt could be very hard. He had to march long distances over harsh desert, carrying his weapons and supplies. Food and water had to be gathered from the land as he traveled. However, there were also big rewards. After a victory, soldiers might share in enemy possessions, such as cattle, weapons, and clothing. The Egyptian soldiers also took some conquered people back to Egypt as slaves.

A warrior who showed courage on the battlefield might even be appointed as an officer. He would be presented with rewards of gold and slaves. Only **noblemen** or well-educated commoners, however, could reach the topmost ranks of the army. Kings often appointed their own sons to command the army divisions.

On the Battlefield

During the period of the New Kingdom, the Egyptian army was organized into four divisions. These were named after the four most important gods—Amun, Re, Ptah *(peh tah)*, and Seth *(sehth)*. Each division contained about 3,000 foot soldiers, as well as numerous archers and chariot drivers. There were also many foreign troops, mostly from other parts of the Egyptian empire, such as Nubia.

In battle, the army's archers sent volleys (many shots released at the same time) of arrows into the enemy ranks. More archers were carried forward on chariots, driven by expert horsemen, to fire at the enemy. Behind them came the infantry, armed with spears, maces (war clubs), battleaxes, or **bronze** swords.

THE COMPOSITE BOW

For many centuries, Egyptian archers used the Nubian longbow, made of wood. This bow was as tall as a man and was said to shoot arrows over 650 feet (200 meters). The New Kingdom archers adopted the **composite** *(kuhm POZ iht)* bow used by the Hyksos. This was made of layers of horn or tendons from animals, glued to a wooden frame and wrapped in bark. The composite bow was much more accurate than the longbow and could shoot arrows about twice as far.

▼ A regiment of carved wooden soldiers on the march dates from around 2000 B.C. The models were found in the tomb of a Middle Kingdom prince. The ancient Egyptians believed that rulers would need armies to protect them in the afterlife, so they often buried model soldiers in royal tombs and those of important officials.

ARTISANS AND CRAFTWORKERS

Many items in ancient Egypt were made by artisans and craftworkers. These workers had small workshops scattered throughout the Nile Valley, where they produced both essential materials and luxury goods. The biggest craft industries were for such everyday objects as mud-bricks, rope, and linen. Both men and women spun flax into thread and wove cloth.

More highly skilled artisans and artists labored on great projects for the pharaoh and the **nobles**. These artisans carved statues, decorated tomb walls with paintings and **relief** carvings (sculptures in which the figures or designs project from their background), and made jewelry and other ornaments.

THE VILLAGE OF TOMB MAKERS

Many pharaohs of the New Kingdom were buried in the Valley of the Kings, near Thebes. A large number of laborers were needed to carve tombs into the rock and decorate them. These laborers lived with their families in a nearby village, Deir el-Medina *(DAIR ehl muh DEE nuh)*. **Archaeologists** have **excavated** the village and discovered a great deal about the lives of the workers and their families. The workers included quarrymen, stonemasons, and painters, as well as the servants who brought supplies, washed clothes, and baked bread for them.

Near this village, several of the workers from Deir el-Medina made elaborate tombs for their families. These were inspired by the grand tombs on which the workers spent their lives.

◀ A wall painting from the tomb of Nefertari *(neh fehr TAHR ee)*, a queen of Ramses II, shows the queen (right) with the goddess Isis. Skilled artisans created such works for the tombs of ancient Egypt.

Potters and Carpenters

Potters had plenty of raw materials close at hand. They mixed clay from the **silt** of the riverbanks and shaped it into anything from bowls and beer jars to beautifully painted vases. Finer pots were made on a wheel, at least in later periods, that the potter turned with one hand while shaping the clay with the other.

Carpenters had simple tools. The Egyptians did not produce iron, so the blades of saws and chisels were usually made of copper, **bronze**, or **flint**. With these tools, carpenters could make furniture, coffins, and even ships. For everyday products, they used local timber, such as the wood of palm trees. For more precious objects, they used higher-quality wood from abroad, especially cedar from Lebanon and **ebony** *(EHB uh nee)* imported from the lands to the south of Egypt.

Working with Stone and Metal

The deserts and hills near the Nile Valley contained large supplies of different kinds of stone. Artisans carved many things from these. Soft stones, such as soapstone and limestone, were made into household items, including bowls, hearths *(hahrthz—the stone floors of fireplaces)*, and troughs *(trawfs)*, or the **canopic** *(kuh NOH pihk)* **jars** found in royal tombs. Harder stones, such as **basalt** *(buh SAWLT)*, might be used for a magnificent **sarcophagus** *(sahr KOF uh guhs)* or statues of gods and rulers.

Metalworkers used copper, gold, and other imported metals. First, they had to purify the metal by separating it from the **ore** in a furnace. Then, workers shaped the metal by melting it and pouring it into a mold or beating it with stone hammers. Gold was much softer, and it could be cut with flint knives and twisted to make ornaments or chains.

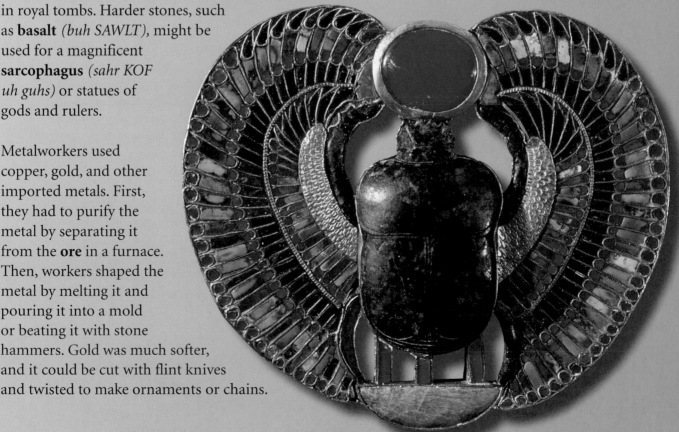

▼ A gold chest ornament in the form of a scarab, or beetle, centered on a winged **sun disk.** The ornament is set with gemstones—including carnelian *(car NEEL yuhn)*, lapis lazuli *(LAP ihs LAZ yuh ly)*, and **turquoise** stones. The ornament was discovered in 1922 in the tomb of Tutankhamun.

FARMERS

Most people in ancient Egypt lived at the edge of the **flood plain** or on higher land along the Nile. The vast majority of these people were peasant farmers or farm laborers. The annual flooding of the Nile and the **fertile** land this created allowed for a huge harvest of crops, which helped to make Egypt a wealthy land. When the rains or the floods were poor, however, there were poor harvests and the whole country suffered.

The farmers lived in villages scattered along the valley. Most had their own small plots of land, but many also worked on the large estates owned by the royal family or by the temples. The landowners usually paid them with a small portion of the crops harvested at the end of the season.

The Gift of the Nile

Egyptian farmers used the light and warmth of the sun, the waters of the Nile, and the fertile **silt** to great success. As soon as the annual floods had subsided in September, the farmers got to work. They planted seeds in the black soil and covered them by pulling a plow across the fields.

THE NILOMETER

The ancient Egyptians kept a close watch on the Nile's yearly flooding. Along the river, from Aswan to the **Delta**, were a series of points now called "Nilometers." In later periods, these were often passages with steps cut down to the river's edge, as in the photo at left. The passages were marked to measure the level of the water. Priests checked these markings at regular intervals to see whether the water was rising. From these readings, they were able to predict the height of the flood for that year and estimate expected income from taxes.

The crops grew quickly in the sun. The farmers watered them by opening up channels leading to ponds where floodwater was stored. They cleared away weeds with hoes. When the crops were mature, the farmers harvested and processed the produce, before storing it or exchanging it for other goods at local markets. But there was still much work to do, including clearing irrigation ditches before the next planting.

▲ An artist's depiction of ancient Egyptian farmers at work beside the Nile River.

Crops and Animals

The main crops grown in ancient Egypt were wheat, barley, and flax (a fibrous plant used for making linen). The pharaoh's tax officials measured the crops and calculated how much tax each farmer would need to pay. Most farmers also grew vegetables, including beans, onions, garlic, and lettuce; and fruit, including melons, pomegranates *(POM GRAN ihts)*, figs, and grapes.

Some farmers kept a few animals, such as goats, geese, and ducks. Cattle were very valuable. Only wealthier farmers could afford to have large herds, which grazed beside the Nile. People gathered extra food by hunting for water birds in the marshes and fishing in the river.

SERVANTS AND SLAVES

The pharaoh and wealthy **noble** families employed a large number of male and female servants. These servants did all the manual labor inside and outside of the palaces and houses. Indoors, servants cleaned, cooked, washed clothes, and waited on their employers. Outdoors, laborers tended the crops and animals, gathered the harvest, and dug the irrigation channels.

The Work of a House Servant

In rich households, those jobs that took the most time and effort usually were done by servants. Every day, for example, servants had to grind grain to make bread. First, they used a grindstone to break up the hard grains. Then they pounded the broken grains into finer flour in a stone bowl. After this, the flour had to be sifted to get rid of husks and grit.

There were many other exhausting jobs. Servants collected fuel—usually dried animal dung or straw—for the fires. They carried large amounts of water from the nearest well or the river. They mixed and baked bread and brewed beer. The mistress of the house watched them carefully to make sure everything was done properly.

SETTING FREE A SLAVE

Sa-Bastet, a royal barber in the reign of Thutmose III (1479–1425 B.C.), wrote a will in which he freed his slave and married him to his niece:

"The slave given to me for my own and whose name is Amenyoiu, I have won him by the force of my arm when I accompanied my king... He shall no longer be stopped at any of the king's gates. I have given him the daughter of my sister Nebetta as wife, who is named Takamenet, and have bequeathed him a portion equal to my wife's and my sister's. As for him, he has emerged from need and is poor no longer."

From a work by French Egyptologist Christiane Desroches Noblecourt, *La femme aux temps des Pharaons*

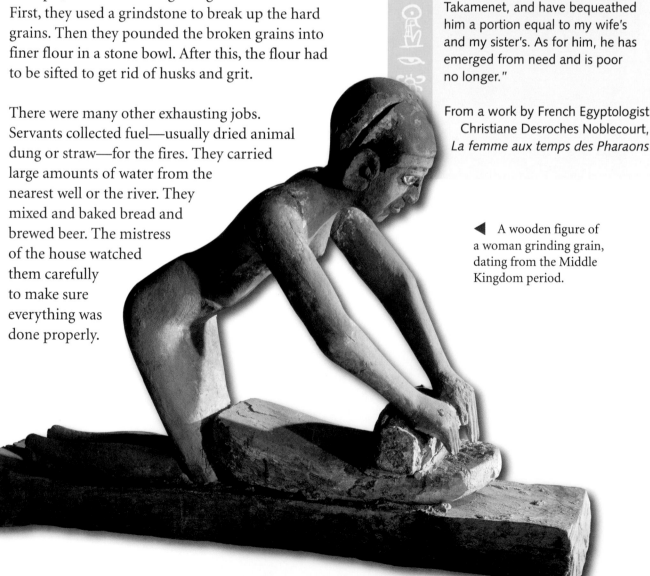

◀ A wooden figure of a woman grinding grain, dating from the Middle Kingdom period.

◀ A painted **relief** on a tomb wall, which dates from between 2450 and 2325 B.C., depicts two servants carrying food. The woman on the left cradles a goat on her forearm and balances a basket of figs on her head; the woman on the right holds a duck by its wing and carries a basket of bread.

Slave Labor

At the bottom of the social scale were slaves. There were large numbers of forced laborers in ancient Egypt, especially during the Middle and New kingdoms. Many slaves were from Asia or central Africa and had been taken as prisoners in wars. Others had sold themselves as slaves to pay off debts.

Slaves had fewer rights than ordinary Egyptians. They were barred from entering or worshiping in shrines and temple courts. They were regarded as items of property and could be bought or sold by their owners. Yet some owners treated their slaves well. They were fed, housed, and supplied with clothes and were allowed to rent plots of land if they could afford it. Many owners also set slaves free to become Egyptian citizens.

BELIEFS, GODS, AND GODDESSES

The religion of the early ancient Egyptians is not as well understood as that of the later periods. Scholars do know that before 3000 B.C., the Egyptians worshiped multiple gods from very early on, and that these gods were often represented as animals or combined animal-human forms. By the time of unification, the ancient Egyptians had developed gods that were local to specific areas.

When all of these various local gods and belief systems came together, the ancient Egyptians were left with many different religious beliefs that explained how the world was created and how it worked. There were a large number of gods and goddesses whom the ancient Egyptians believed watched over this world, controlling and influencing all that people did and how nature behaved. In each district or town, however, people continued to worship their own local gods, though they also accepted and worshiped the major gods of Egypt.

▼ A detail from a painted coffin—dating from around 984 B.C.—shows the sun god Re traveling in his boat across the sky, about to kill the serpent of darkness. The Egyptians believed that each morning Re killed the serpent in order to be able to rise in the east.

The Major Gods

During the time of the Middle Kingdom, when rulers from Thebes controlled the country, the Egyptians worshiped a sun god called Amun, in addition to other national and local gods. In time, Amun merged with Re, also a sun god, as the single deity—Amun-Re. By the time of the New Kingdom, the main god of the ancient Egyptians was Re, also known as Ra *(rah).*

The most important female god was Isis *(EYE sihs),* who was goddess of mothers, wives, and other aspects of life, including birth and growth. She is often shown as a woman wearing a headdress of cow horns with a **sun disk.** Her brother Osiris *(oh SY rihs)* ruled over the afterlife and the dead. Osiris is usually shown as a bearded human **mummy** with green or black skin. Isis and Osiris also had a son called Horus *(HAWR uhs),* who was a god of the sky and kingship. Artists painted Horus as either a falcon or a falcon-headed man.

JUDGING THE DEAD

Osiris, chief god of the underworld, judged the dead and decided their fate in the afterlife. In this image from the ***Book of the Dead,*** Osiris (above, far left) is shown on his throne, sitting in judgment, while the heart of a dead person is weighed on scales. If the heart of the dead person (whose spirit is depicted at furthest right) was weighted down with wrongdoing, it would be heavier than a feather from the goddess of truth, Ma'at *(mah aht),* seen standing directly in front of the spirit. If the heart weighed less than the feather, the deceased could enter the underworld. But if the heart weighed more than the feather, it was devoured by the monster Ammit *(ah mit),* who had the head and hindquarters of a crocodile, and the body of a lion. Thoth, Anubis, and Horus (center, from left to right) were also thought to be present at this judgment. Some paintings show the dead condemned in this **ritual** being punished for eternity, while in other sources the dead person was thought to cease existence once condemned.

Mummies and the Afterlife

Ancient Egyptians believed that when a person died, his or her spirit was released from the body. In order to have a good afterlife, the spirit needed to come back to its body. **Mummification** was developed as a way to preserve a dead body well enough to allow it to be recognizable and usable for the spirit after death.

The Afterlife and the Need for Mummies

A **mummy** is a dead body that has been preserved and that still has some of its soft tissue—that is, a body that has decayed only to a limited degree. This can happen naturally in a very dry climate or can be done artificially.

Before around 3000 B.C., most people in ancient Egypt were buried in the ground when they died. In the hot, dry conditions, bodies remained well preserved and often were naturally mummified. Later, however, kings and **nobles** began to be buried in mastabas (*MAHS tuh buhz*)—tombs made out of dried brick. Mastabas had a chamber below ground to hold the body. In later examples, above ground was another room designed to receive the offerings left for the dead. By around 3000 B.C., just as the belief in the need for a person's body to achieve an afterlife became widespread, the royalty and nobility of Egypt were being buried in a coffin placed within a tomb instead of in the sand. With this change, the Egyptians began to invent ways to preserve bodies.

Preserving the Body

To preserve the dead, the Egyptians **embalmed** (*ehm BAHLMED*) and dried corpses to stop them from decaying. In the usual process of mummification, embalmers

▶ One of a set of four canopic jars used to preserve the internal organs of an Egyptian prince in the 800's B.C. The **hieroglyphic** text on the front is addressed to the goddess Isis, asking for her protection.

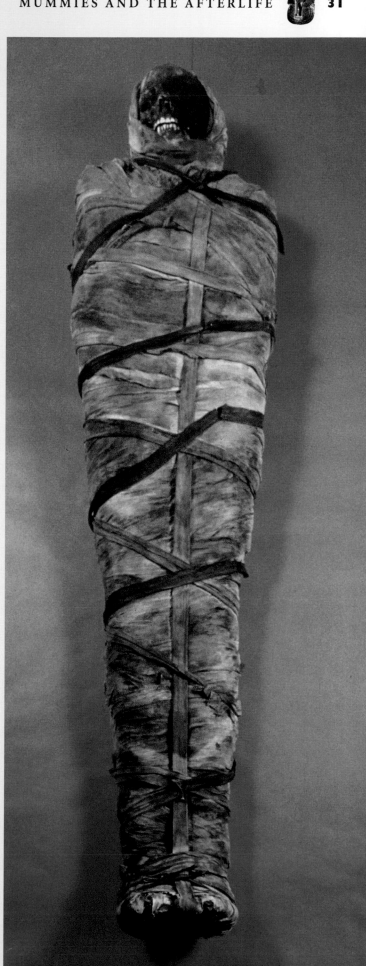

would cut open the body and remove the lungs, liver, stomach, and intestines of the dead. The organs were dried with a natural salt, **natron** *(NAY tron)*, which drew out the moisture from the organs. Ordinarily, the organs were then stored separately in stone jars, called **canopic jars.** During certain periods, however, the organs were wrapped in parcels and placed back inside of the body or put into one parcel and placed on top of the body. Embalmers also removed the brain. Usually, they used a long rod with a small spoon-shaped device to pull the brain out through the nose. The brain tissue was just discarded.

The embalmers placed natron inside the corpse and covered what remained of the corpse with natron. The body was allowed to dry for about 40 days. Once the body was dried, it could be stuffed with straw, linen, moss, or some other material to give it a more lifelike shape. It was coated with spices and lotions. Then, the body was wrapped in layers of linen strips. As the mummy was being wrapped, a priest read aloud spells to launch the dead person on his or her journey to the afterlife. **Amulets** *(AM yuh lihtz)*, a kind of charm, were also placed in the wrappings. The entire process of mummification could take as long as 70 days.

▶ The mummy of a teenage Egyptian girl who lived between the 1200's and 1000's B.C.

ONLY FOR THE RICH
By around 2600 B.C., the elaborate process of mummification had become a profitable business, and only those whose families could afford to pay for it were preserved in this way.

MUMMIES AND THE AFTERLIFE

For the spirits of the dead to exist in the afterlife, they needed bodies to which they could return. In addition, the dead needed food, drink, and possessions to live on. These requirements led to complex **mortuary** practices.

Taking No Chances

Before the process of **mummification** was perfected, a dead person's spirit needed something it could use to identify its own body or could use if its body was destroyed. This need for a means of identification may have led to the use of reserve heads. These were heads modeled of stone to look like the deceased person and placed next to the tomb. However, scholars are unsure about the exact purpose of these stone heads, and they were not made after around 2500 B.C.

Even after mummification made it likely that a corpse would survive in a recognizable form, the Egyptians feared something would go wrong that might lead to the loss of an afterlife. By the Middle Kingdom, coffins featured paintings that resembled the deceased. All these likenesses of the dead person were thought to help the soul identify its corpse.

Tomb statues came into use as another way to ensure an afterlife. The statue of a human figure, usually made of stone or wood, had the name of the dead person inscribed upon it, in the belief that this would enable the person's spirit to find the right tomb. The ancient Egyptians also believed the statue could be used as a body if anything happened to destroy the **mummy.** By the Middle Kingdom, this practice was widespread for both the upper and middle classes.

▼ Carved wooden models, dating from around 1950 B.C., of a procession of servants carrying offerings. Such models were put in tombs to magically perform the work of living servants.

▶ The funerary (death) boat of Khufu *(KOO foo)*, an Old Kingdom king, who ruled from around 2589 to 2566 B.C. The boat had been buried near Khufu's tomb, the Great **Pyramid** at Giza. After the boat was discovered, it was reassembled and placed in a museum at the site.

Model Servants

Because mummies required food and drink, their families and—for important people and royalty—priests, would take daily offerings to their mortuary temples or offering chapels. In fact, certain groups of priests were sometimes put under contract to bring offerings to the temple of a ruler or the chapel of a **noble** forever.

Still, Egyptians worried that over time their bodies would be deprived of the things they needed. The belief arose that something in a tomb representing an object could magically become the object itself. At certain periods, elaborate scenes were painted on tomb walls. The paintings might depict food or drink that the dead could magically consume. Alternatively, the paintings were sometimes of everyday events and pastimes, to provide the dead with something enjoyable to do.

Eventually, models were also created to serve this purpose. These models could be of food, of small human figures intended to act as servants, of weapons to allow the dead to protect themselves, or of anything else the dead might need.

THE OPENING OF THE MOUTH

Because the ancient Egyptians believed that a dead person's soul needed food and drink to survive in the afterlife, priests at a burial performed a special Opening of the Mouth **ritual**. They believed this ritual allowed the dead to receive nourishment. The Opening of the Mouth required special tools—including ritual knives and **amulets**—and priests chanting spells over the coffin that held the corpse.

PYRAMID TOMBS

The most famous buildings of ancient Egypt—the **pyramids**—were built as tombs. The pyramids are some of the oldest and largest stone structures in the world. The ruins of more than 35 major pyramids still stand along the Nile. Most were the tombs of kings, but some smaller pyramids held the remains of favored members of the royal family or the nobility.

The major pyramids were built from around 2600 B.C. to 1700 B.C. After that time, the royal families began to be entombed inside chambers within the cliffs at such sites as the Valley of the Kings and the Valley of the Queens, both near Thebes. These valleys were easier to guard against tomb robbers.

Building a Pyramid

It was vital to choose the right site for a pyramid. The site had to be flat and stable enough to bear the enormous weight of the stone used in the pyramid. Once the site was chosen, the outline of the pyramid was marked out. Then, workmen dug the underground chambers, halls, and stairs. Only after that could the vast job of building the pyramid above ground begin. For this part of the building, thousands of stone blocks had to be moved from the **quarry** to the building site. These stones were either dragged to the site or brought by boat.

▲ The Step Pyramid, built as the tomb for King Zoser *(zoh zer)* in about 2650 B.C., was one of the first large pyramids.

TOMB ROBBERS

The tomb makers tried to hide the entrances to pyramids and tombs. Nevertheless, robbers found their way in. Some raided tombs in the Valley of the Kings soon after they were sealed. They tunneled or broke through the entrance and took away objects made of gold and silver, linen clothing, and other valuable items. Tomb makers added many tricks and traps to fool the robbers. Some passages ended in blank walls or had pits for intruders to fall into. Despite these efforts, most royal tombs were raided, and the precious contents taken.

Egyptian builders had only simple tools, such as wooden squares, stone hammers, and saws and drills made of copper and **bronze**. With these, they cut through granite and **basalt**, some of the hardest stones in the world.

The core of a pyramid was usually made of rough-shaped chunks of limestone packed together; the chambers inside were lined with granite or basalt. The outer casing was usually also made of limestone and cut smooth. As the pyramid grew higher, some **archaeologists** think laborers built ramps of mud so that the blocks could be hauled up to the next level. Once the pyramid was complete, the ramps were removed.

Muscle Power

The raising of a pyramid needed huge numbers of laborers. Some archaeologists calculate that a regular force of 25,000 men worked on the building of the Great Pyramid at Giza over a period of more than 20 years. On average, the workers were laying more than 300 stone blocks every day.

While it was once thought that the pyramids were built by slaves, scholars now think that the pyramids were built by skilled work teams who oversaw corvee *(kawr VAY)* workers—people drafted by the Egyptian government to serve in the army or on building projects.

▼ The **Sphinx**, an enormous carving of a lion with the head of a man, stands before the Great Pyramid of Khufu, built between 2600 and 2500 B.C. The head and body of the Sphinx were carved directly from a giant rock, to which cut stone blocks were added to form legs. The outer layer of smooth, white stone that once covered the Great Pyramid has largely been reused to build later structures.

TEMPLES

▲ Vast columns at the ruin of the Temple of Amun in Karnak. The temple was built in the early 1300's B.C.

Two basic kinds of temples existed in ancient Egypt: temples at which a god was worshiped and **mortuary temples**, where the **cult** of a dead person, usually a king or queen, was celebrated. Of course, kings and queens were considered to be gods, so it is perhaps a small distinction.

Offerings were given to the god being celebrated at a temple. A statue of the god was also housed and cared for in the temple. In fact, the word for temple, *hut-nutjer (huht NEHT juhr)*, meant "mansion of the god." (See also pages 18 through 19 for information about temple **rituals**.)

Temples in ancient Egypt were often large buildings made of stone, as were the **pyramids.** Except for pyramids and temples, the Egyptians tended to build most buildings of less durable materials, such as mud-brick. This is why there are few examples of these other kinds of buildings from ancient Egypt still standing.

Most temples were built according to the same basic plan and had the same elements. Many temples were built beside the Nile, so most temples had a small dock that allowed people traveling by boat, bringing statues of gods from neighboring temples, to visit. A temple and its grounds were surrounded by walls. The grounds could include a sacred lake and smaller temples and shrines.

Outside all temple gates were sets of flagstaffs. The flag on a flagstaff informed visitors which god was in residence at the temple, much as flags outside modern palaces in the United Kingdom inform visitors whether or not the queen is in residence. At the entrance to a temple was a gateway, usually formed of two huge towers, which scholars call pylons *(PY lonz)*. Beyond the pylons was usually a courtyard with columns around its outer edge. Beyond this courtyard was a series of halls, also with columns. Beyond the halls were small chambers, known as **sanctuaries**. In one of these small chambers, the statue of the god was kept. Only priests were allowed to enter the sanctuaries.

These huge and important temples owned large amounts of land and livestock, and had a great many priests and officials working for them.

TEMPLE SIGNS AND SYMBOLS

The objects and architecture of a temple held meaning for the ancient Egyptians. The flagstaff that was always at the entrance of a temple had been in front of temples even in early times when they were small buildings made of reeds or mud and sticks. The **hieroglyph** for the Egyptian word *netjer,* meaning "god," was a symbol showing a flag on a staff. The shape of a pylon looked like the hieroglyph for *horizon,* where the Egyptians believed the sun was reborn each day. The sanctuary, where the god's image was kept, was the highest point in most temples and thus symbolized the mound of creation. The temple was carefully constructed to represent creation, rebirth, and the gods.

◄ Colossal *(kuh LOS uhl)*, or gigantic, statues—these measure 130 feet (40 meters) high and 13 feet (4 meters) from ear to ear—flank the entrance to the Great Temple of Ramses II. In the 1960's, this temple was relocated from the shores of the Nile because its location was going to be flooded when the Aswan Dam was completed. The front of the temple, including the four giant statues on either side of the entrance, had been carved from natural rock. To be moved, it all had to be sawn into pieces and then lifted to higher ground. The project took four years to complete.

LANGUAGE AND WRITING

Writing developed very early in the history of ancient Egypt. By around 3100 B.C. and possibly even as early as 3200 B.C., the **hieroglyphic** script was already being used. At the start of the Old Kingdom, Egyptians had invented a kind of paper made from the **papyrus** plant. By this time, trained **scribes** were using a well-established system of writing.

These developments were vital in helping the rulers to establish a strong central government. With writing, officials were able to record such information as the dates of reigns, the names of kings and queens, important events, and calculations of taxes. These records were inscribed on stones, pressed into wet clay, or painted on walls and papyrus rolls. Writing also played a major role in such **rituals** as funerals.

▼ A stone figure of a scribe, dating from the 2450's B.C., was found in a tomb. The scribe sits cross-legged with a roll of papyrus on his lap, ready to write.

Hieroglyphs

Egyptian writing had no alphabet in the modern sense. Instead, the scribes used hieroglyphs. This was a system of picture symbols, which represented different ideas and sounds. The word hieroglyph comes from the Greek name for Egyptian writing and means *sacred carving*. According to later Egyptian myth, the script had been invented by Thoth *(thohth)*, the god of wisdom.

The earliest hieroglyphic signs were simple pictures of objects that Egyptians could easily recognize, such as a woman, snake, or bird. Scribes also had single signs for more complex things, such as ideas. In addition, they used some symbols to represent individual sounds. By combining two or more of these sound signs, scribes were able to build many new written words.

The Work of a Scribe

A scribe had to go through a long and thorough training. Boys usually began attending a scribal school at the age of 10. They had to learn a huge number of different signs (during some periods, there were as many as 700 signs). After completing their training, the young boy went to work for a master scribe. Some girls were also trained as scribes, though this was not common.

▲ Hieroglyphs on papyrus from the *Book of the Dead.*

THE ROSETTA STONE

Western scholars' deciphering (discovering the meaning) of ancient Egypt's language began when the French general Napoleon Bonaparte invaded Egypt. In 1799, his soldiers found a black rock covered in three kinds of writing, including ancient Greek. The French scholar Jean-François Champollion *(zhahn frahn swah shahn paw lyawn)* discovered the stone contained the same message written in three languages. By using the Greek version (still used today) and building on the earlier work of the British scholar Thomas Young, Champollion worked out the meanings of many Egyptian words. British troops later removed the stone. It has been in the British Museum in London since 1802, although many modern Egyptians feel it should be returned to Egypt.

A scribe's tools and equipment were simple. He sat on a mat, with a roll of papyrus on his knees. To make a pen or brush, he took a piece of rush (a kind of grass) and chewed the end to splay out the fibers. He had a wooden palette with hollows for holding the cakes of paint (usually just black and red) and a small pot of water for wetting the brushes.

▼ Two of the three scripts on part of the Rosetta Stone that allowed hieroglyphic writing to be deciphered.

PAINTING AND SCULPTURE

The ancient Egyptians did not think of painters, sculptors, and other decorative workers as being creative artists. They saw them simply as **artisans** or craftworkers, whose job was to produce images of people and animals. Artisans and artists had to follow the instructions given to them by the architect or chief official in charge of the project. They were not encouraged to create original art of their own.

Most jobs assigned to artisans and artists were connected with religion, because religion was at the center of ancient Egyptian life. Painters, sculptors, jewelers, and others worked together in workshops near the palace or where their creations were needed, such as at the site of a **pyramid** or temple.

Painting the Walls

One of the most important tasks of a painter was to decorate the walls inside tombs or temples. The subjects might be the life and achievements of the dead person, his or her meetings with gods and goddesses, or even the funeral ceremonies and the procession itself.

First, the draftsmen drew a grid of vertical and horizontal lines to guide them. Then they drew the outline of the picture, usually in ink. Next, sculptors might cut out the shapes using a chisel to make a shallow kind of carving called **relief.** The painters added color to the pictures with rush or hair brushes. They mixed their paints with water and then with egg white or gum to make them smoother and to help the paint to stick well.

A Sculptor at Work

Sculptors usually carved figures from softer stone, such as limestone or sandstone. The soft stone allowed them to use the same tools as woodworkers, which were made of copper or **bronze**. To shape hard stone, they used hammers made of even harder pebbles.

▼ A painted limestone statue of a young boy reveals the skill of ancient Egyptian sculptors. The statue was found at Saqqarah and dates from around 2500 B.C.

▲ A painted relief, dated around 1290 B.C., from the walls of the tomb of Ramses I in the Valley of the Kings. The pharaoh is shown kneeling between Horus (left), the falcon-headed god of kingship, and Anubis (right), the jackal-headed god of the dead.

Large pieces of stone could also be cracked by lighting fires on them (to heat the stone) and then pouring on water to put out the fires. The quick change in temperature would split the stone.

Artisans often decorated stone statues with paint and other materials. Faces, hands, and feet were painted in flesh colors, and clothing was usually white. Carved ornaments might be covered in gold leaf (thin sheets of gold). Some statues had lifelike eyes made of hard white stone or crystal set in copper.

SEEN FROM TWO SIDES

The people in ancient Egyptian paintings can look strange to us because they are shown very differently from modern styles. The head is drawn in profile (turned to the side), but the eye is shown in full. The legs turn the same way as the head, but the **torso** is seen from the front. The artists wanted to show the whole of a person's body, not just part of it from a single angle. Scholars think the ancient Egyptians believed that by depicting the whole body, they would preserve it for eternity.

FAMILY LIFE

The family was very important to the ancient Egyptians and was at the center of many religious **rituals**. A man was expected to set up house with his wife, who ran the household, and they would have children as soon as they could. He was the head of the household, and he needed a son to take over his position after his death.

Being part of a family was also vital for a person's afterlife. When someone died, their spirit was thought to live on with the body in the tomb, but only if the tomb was properly looked after. For common people, the children and other relatives took on the important duty of arranging the funeral and tending their parents' spirits by giving regular offerings and saying the correct spells.

Women

Ancient Egyptian women lived much more freely than women in many other parts of the ancient world. According to the law, women had many of the same rights as men. Women could buy and sell property, sign contracts, and bring lawsuits against other people. Married women could also choose to divorce their husbands.

Women were free to go out in public. Many of them worked in the fields with their husbands, in workshops, and in the markets. It was common for women to work washing clothes or making linen cloth and garments. Upper-class women often held a religious position at the local temple or shrine as singers or dancers.

◀ A chair, a stool, baskets, and other household items made by the ancient Egyptians of wood, rushes, and palm leaves. These items date from the mid-1500's to the late 1200's B.C.

▲ A family portrait of Bechu, at far left, and his wife, who is seated between two sons. The statue, carved from stone and painted, was made between 1539 and 1075 B.C.

Everyday Housework

Most Egyptian families rose early before the day had grown hot. The men usually went to work in the fields or in workshops. At harvest time, women often helped their husbands to bring in the crops. But usually the women had a lot of work to do in the home. There was grain to grind, bread and beer to make, and children to look after.

Cleaning the house was another important part of the daily routine. Floors were usually made of pounded earth. Women sprinkled water to dampen the dust, then swept the floors with brushes made of reeds or palm fibers. Cleanliness was vital because there was no drainage system in commoners' houses until around 30 B.C. Household garbage was thrown on a pile nearby or into the river. Rats, flies, and disease could thrive in the hot climate, so it was important to dispose of things far away from one's home.

Children and Childbirth

Many children died very young in the ancient world, owing to disease or other problems. Experts have estimated that at least one child in every three died at a young age in Egypt. Even so, Egyptian families were often large, with an average of four or more children.

NAMING A CHILD

Babies were given their names as soon as they were born. The first name was sometimes connected to the happiness of the event or to the way the child behaved, such as *Joyful* or *Strong.* The parents might also give the child the name of a god or goddess, in the hope that this would give them special protection from harm.

SHELTER AND CLOTHING

There were many settlements in the Nile Valley. During the New Kingdom, **archaeologists** believe there were more than 3 million people living there. They built on high ground to avoid the annual flooding. Egyptians generally constructed their homes out of sun-dried mud-bricks. They used the trunks of palm trees to support the flat roofs.

These towns and villages usually developed in an apparently unplanned way, with narrow streets and houses jumbled together around the market place, the temple, and other public buildings. Only a few settlements were carefully planned, with straight streets and houses all in a row.

Houses of the Rich and Poor

Nobles and wealthy officials could afford to have large homes. These grand homes might have as many as 70 rooms, often ornately decorated and richly furnished. Outside there was space for large gardens and outbuildings, including a pool or fishpond and a family shrine.

▲ A clay model of an Egyptian house, made around 1900 B.C. The center arch is the entrance; the archway to the left leads to stairs or a ramp to the roof, where people slept on hot nights. Such models were placed in tombs to represent the former dwelling of the dead.

WIGS

Many Egyptian men and women wore their hair short or completely shaved off. On special occasions, such as festivals, they often wore wigs made of human hair and vegetable fibers. In some periods, to hold their wigs in place, women fixed a headband round their foreheads.

Most ordinary Egyptians lived in small houses. The poorest of all had only one-room huts. A better-off craftworker might have a house of three or more rooms, with two stories. Keeping cool was sometimes difficult, so Egyptian houses featured small windows set high in the wall to help keep out the sun. There was often a staircase to the roof, where people climbed up to sleep on very hot nights. The cooking was done outside, away from the house.

Clothes and Cosmetics

Egyptians generally dressed in clothes made of white linen. In hot weather, men wore little more than a short, skirtlike garment wrapped round the waist. Women wore simple robes or dresses with shoulder straps (see the image on page 51). In winter, many people wore linen or hide cloaks. Wealthier people had leather sandals, but most Egyptians usually went barefoot.

Egyptians used cosmetics. Women colored their nails with a reddish-brown dye. They also used red lip-powder. Both men and women lined their eyes with a black make-up called *kohl;* the Egyptians may also have believed that kohl protected them against eye disease. Because of the harshness of the sun, many people used lotions to keep their skin soft. These lotions were made of scented animal or vegetable oils.

▶ The top half of a pleated dress for a woman from ancient Egypt. Dating to around 3000 B.C., the dress is thought to be the oldest preserved garment in the world.

FOOD AND DRINK

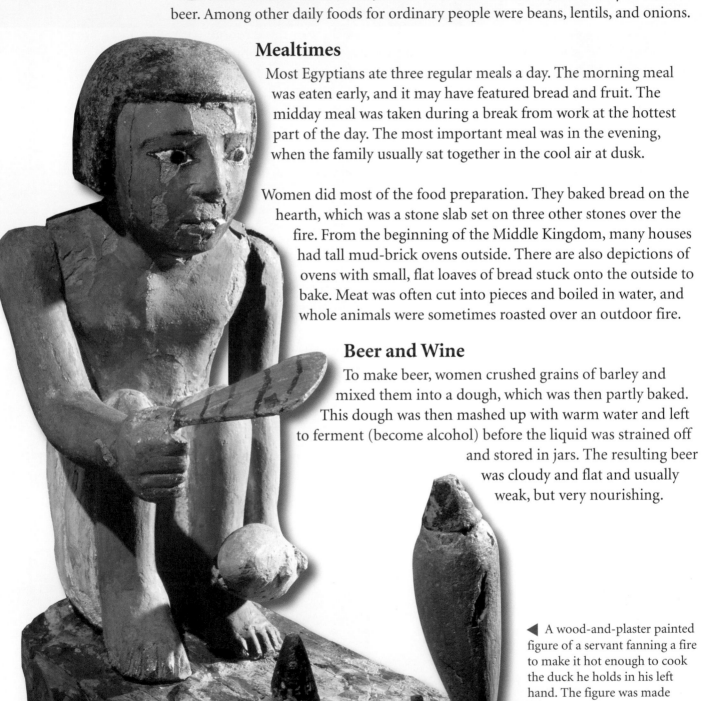

Grains were among the most important crops in ancient Egypt. The Egyptians used wheat to make bread, which was their main food, and barley to make beer. Among other daily foods for ordinary people were beans, lentils, and onions.

Mealtimes

Most Egyptians ate three regular meals a day. The morning meal was eaten early, and it may have featured bread and fruit. The midday meal was taken during a break from work at the hottest part of the day. The most important meal was in the evening, when the family usually sat together in the cool air at dusk.

Women did most of the food preparation. They baked bread on the hearth, which was a stone slab set on three other stones over the fire. From the beginning of the Middle Kingdom, many houses had tall mud-brick ovens outside. There are also depictions of ovens with small, flat loaves of bread stuck onto the outside to bake. Meat was often cut into pieces and boiled in water, and whole animals were sometimes roasted over an outdoor fire.

Beer and Wine

To make beer, women crushed grains of barley and mixed them into a dough, which was then partly baked. This dough was then mashed up with warm water and left to ferment (become alcohol) before the liquid was strained off and stored in jars. The resulting beer was cloudy and flat and usually weak, but very nourishing.

◀ A wood-and-plaster painted figure of a servant fanning a fire to make it hot enough to cook the duck he holds in his left hand. The figure was made around 2040 B.C.

▲ A wall painting from the tomb of a **nobleman** depicts him hunting water birds using a throwing stick. On the boat with him are his wife (right), daughter (center), and a cat (left), jumping to retrieve a catch. The painting dates from the late 1300's B.C.

The Egyptians also made wine from different kinds of fruits, including grapes, figs, and dates. Workers crushed the fruits by treading on them and then strained the juice into open vats before leaving it to ferment. When the wine was ready, it was stored in clay jars stopped with rush plugs and sealed with mud.

HUNTING AND FISHING

The Nile River was a rich source of wild food. The river and floodwater basins were full of fish, which Egyptians caught with nets, hooked lines, or spears. Some of the fish was dried in the sun, preserved in salt, and stored for later use. Hunters killed water birds in the marshes using throwing sticks, or they trapped the birds in nets. There was also plenty of game in the surrounding hills and deserts, including a small antelope known as a gazelle (guh ZEHL) and a kind of wild goat known as an ibex (EYE behks).

CHILDREN AND EDUCATION

Among common people, mothers carried young babies with them while they worked, even in the fields. They usually rested the children on their hips, and supported them with a sling tied round the neck. Disease, accidents, and other dangers were never far away in ancient Egypt. To keep their children safe, mothers tied **amulets** to parts of a child's body. These amulets were an appeal to the gods who protected the different parts of the body. The Egyptians believed that Re, for example, looked after the crown of the head, and Horus looked after the arms.

Games, Toys, and Pets

As soon as young children could walk, they were allowed to play outside. At this age, many children wore no clothes during the heat of the day. However, in the cool evenings, boys probably wore loincloths, and girls wore short dresses. They wrestled, raced, and played leapfrog. As they grew older, boys played more complex games, including mock battles with sticks and swimming races.

◀ A wall painting shows the son of Ramses III wearing the sidelock of youth, standing behind his father.

THE SIDELOCK OF YOUTH

Boys and girls had their hair cut short or completely shaved, except for a lock of hair on the right side of the head. This was called the sidelock of youth and was a sign that they were still children. The lock was braided and curled at the end. It was generally worn until the child was about 14 years of age.

Children played with all sorts of toys that would still be recognized today. They had board games, clay dolls, and leather balls stuffed with straw. Children in wealthier families had wooden toy animals.

Many households also kept animals, particularly dogs, monkeys, and cats, as pets. The Egyptians loved pets, and **archaeologists** have found many mummified domestic animals, especially cats. The Egyptian owners wanted to protect the remains of their pet after its death.

Education

Very few boys and girls went to school in ancient Egypt. From around the age of 5, most children were expected to learn the life skills they needed by helping their parents. They fed farm animals, sowed seed, hoed crops, or took part in the harvest. Children of **artisans** and craftworkers might help in the workshops. Most girls stayed at home to do the housework with their mothers.

Only children from wealthy families went to school. The most common type of education was the kind given to **scribes**. Schools for scribes were usually run by temple priests or by a government department. The students learned to write by copying letters, stories, or business accounts. They practiced writing on **papyrus,** wooden tablets, pieces of broken clay pots, or chips of limestone.

▶ A game table made of pottery and inlaid glass in the shape of a hippopotamus, made between 945 and 715 B.C. The holes in the table and the jackal-headed stick were for the playing of a popular game, 58 holes.

MUSIC, GAMES, AND FESTIVALS

The ancient Egyptians worked hard but also found time to enjoy themselves with banquets, sports, and country outings. Many of these leisure activities are shown in paintings on tomb walls. Of course, there were also more solemn occasions, such as funerals, which featured music and dancing in addition to mourning.

Religious festivals marked special times in the Egyptian year. Some festivals celebrated important events, such as the beginning of the Nile flooding. People gathered on the riverbanks and threw offerings of flowers and food into the water. Other festivals celebrated the different gods. The images of the gods and goddesses were carried in procession, and feasts were held.

Music and Dance

Music and dance were an important part of the entertainment at banquets, temple ceremonies, or in the home. The dancers were usually groups of young girls who moved together in carefully rehearsed patterns. We know very little about how the music sounded, because no written music has been found. For most of ancient Egyptian history, music was played by groups of two or three musicians.

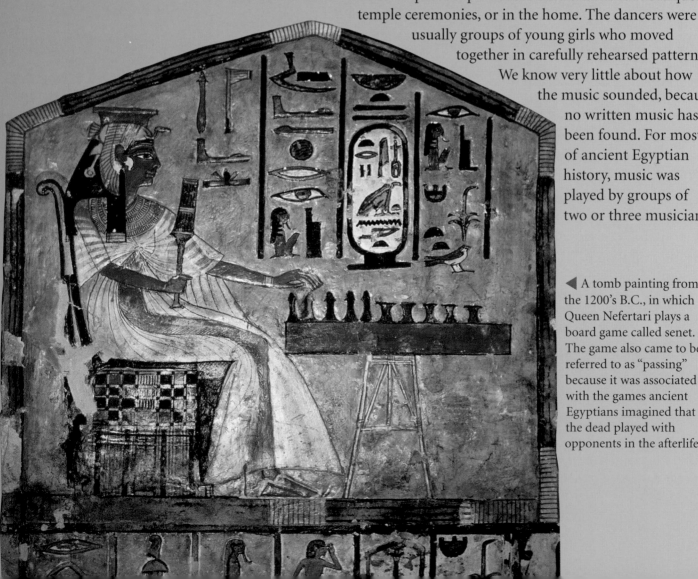

◀ A tomb painting from the 1200's B.C., in which Queen Nefertari plays a board game called senet. The game also came to be referred to as "passing" because it was associated with the games ancient Egyptians imagined that the dead played with opponents in the afterlife.

The main stringed instruments were the harp and the lute, which had a body made of wood or a whole shell from a terrapin (a kind of freshwater or salt-marsh turtle). There were also flutes made of wood or metal. Dancers kept time by stamping and clicking wooden clappers. Singers in temple **rituals** used a rattle called a sistrum (see the image on page 18).

▲ A reproduction of a wall painting from a tomb shows a group of female musicians playing a harp, a lute, a double reed, and a lyre, while a child (center) dances.

Games and Sports

Egyptians enjoyed playing games at home with boards, dice, and marbles. Some of these games are among the oldest in history. One very popular game was senet *(SEHN uht)*, a board game similar to modern backgammon. Two players moved their pieces on a board with 30 squares.

The Nile River was the center of many leisure activities. People liked to swim or fish there or sail small boats. There were also several spectator sports in ancient Egypt. Wrestling matches between trained fighters were often the highlight of a banquet or festival.

THE RITUAL OF HEB SED

A special festival called Heb Sed *(hehb sehd)* was usually held when a pharaoh had ruled for 30 years. This was a celebration, and it included a ritual in which the ruler ran between two markers of stone set at each end of the **court**. These are thought to have represented the lands of Upper and Lower Egypt.

TRADE AND TRANSPORTATION

Ancient Egyptian merchants traveled long distances to exchange Egyptian-made goods for foreign goods. Merchants went overland and via the Red Sea to places in the south, such as Nubia. Some sailed to the ports of the Aegean, Mediterranean, and Red seas, possibly going as far as India, Greece, and even present-day France in later periods.

Many foreign traders also came to Egypt to sell their goods. Middle Kingdom tomb paintings show, for instance, bearded merchants from the region along the eastern Mediterranean and from other parts of the Middle East bringing cosmetics, metal weapons, and leather products. Another group, called the Hyksos by the Egyptians, began migrating into Egypt in the 1700's B.C. and later moved around the **Delta** region and established trading centers.

Raw Materials

Egypt had its own supplies of many important minerals, as well as grain and **papyrus**. But the country lacked some of the raw materials that were vital for building or for making tools and other goods. Rulers sent expeditions abroad to obtain these supplies. Sometimes, they had to send soldiers as well, to conquer regions where the materials were found, or to protect the merchants and miners from attack.

Traders brought back silver, iron, and cedar logs from areas of southwest Asia such as Syria and Lebanon.

◄ A model of a sailboat and its crew, made between 1991 and 1786 B.C. The pilot stands in the bow, dropping the line and anchor. The boat's owner sits in the shade under the canopy.

◀ A wall painting from around the early 1400's B.C. depicts foreign servants bringing tribute to the Egyptian pharaoh, including cattle, water fowl, and jugs of wine.

The Sinai desert region to the northeast was a vital source of **turquoise** and other important minerals. From Nubia, they brought **ivory**, copper, animal skins, and gold.

Boats and Sledges

The main route for transportation was the Nile River. The earliest Egyptian boats were made of papyrus reeds and propelled by poles or oars. By the Old Kingdom (about 2650 to 2150 B.C.), Egyptians had developed sailboats built of reed and timber. These were strong enough to carry loads of stone blocks for the construction of the **pyramids**.

On land, goods were usually carried on sledges—flat wooden platforms—pulled by oxen or men. Carts with wheels were developed during the New Kingdom (about 1539 to 1075 B.C.). Ordinary Egyptians walked or rode donkeys everywhere. Wealthy people might be carried in special chairs called litters.

THE LAND OF PUNT

Relief carvings from the temple of Queen Hatshepsut provide evidence of what happened on one particular Egyptian trading expedition. In about 1496 B.C, this expedition went to the land Egyptians called Punt *(poont)*, possibly in eastern Africa, in present-day Somalia. The pictures show a ship being loaded with exotic goods, including incense *(IHN sehns)* trees in pots, leopard skins, and a troop of baboons. A later picture shows the baboons having escaped and climbed into the rigging.

DECLINE AND CIVIL WAR

Ancient Egypt's power began to weaken during **Dynasty** XX, in around 1200 B.C. There was a bitter struggle for control between the **nobles** and the priests, and the royal rulers were too weak to take charge. The country broke up into small states, which fought against each other in several civil wars.

Egypt lost its territories abroad and soon became vulnerable to invaders. Armies from Libya, Nubia, and other neighboring lands seized parts of Egyptian territory. At the same time, bands of fierce fighters, known as the Sea People, began raiding the eastern borders of Egypt. Scholars do not know where the Sea People came from, but their attempts to settle on the coast of the eastern Mediterranean caused much conflict.

▲ A grey granite carving of the head of King Taharqa, the last Nubian ruler of Egypt.

Collapse of an Empire

Ramses III, one of the last great Egyptian rulers, fought against the invaders. However, his reign ended in about 1156 B.C., when he was probably murdered. Dynasty XX itself ended in around 1075 B.C. Egypt became a lawless place, where bands of foreign soldiers roamed. Robbers broke into the royal tombs at Thebes and stole most of the contents.

The history of ancient Egypt during this period is not clear, because the records are poor or have been lost. Many different leaders took control and then fell. Among them was Shoshenq *(shoh SHEHNKH)* I, who unified the country again for a short time in about 940 B.C. Another was Piankhy *(pee AHNKH eye)*, a Nubian leader, who conquered southern Egypt as far as Memphis by about 730 B.C. The Nubians would rule Egypt for nearly 100 years. The "black pharaohs" of Nubia combined their own **culture** with Egyptian customs that they admired.

The last of the Nubian pharaohs was Taharqa *(tuh HAR quh)*, who was counted as a great military commander. Eventually, Taharqa lost Egypt to invaders beginning with battles that started in the

Timeline of Later Egyptian History

around 1075 B.C. The end of Dynasty XX; renewed civil war and extensive political and social change in Egypt

around 940 B.C. Libyan king Shoshenq I founds Dynasty XXII and restores control briefly

around 730 B.C. Nubian king Piankhy builds empire in southern Egypt

around 665 B.C. Assyrians invade Egypt and sack Thebes

525 B.C. Persians drive out the Assyrians and take control

332 B.C. Alexander defeats the Persians; beginning of Greek rule

323 B.C. Death of Alexander; Ptolemy fights to rule Egypt

51 B.C. Cleopatra VII becomes ruler of Egypt

31 B.C. Death of Cleopatra and Antony; Egypt becomes a province of Rome

▲ Small mud-brick pyramids in present-day Sudan, built in about 700 B.C.

670's B.C. Taharqa continued to rule Nubia after this, however, and was buried in a **pyramid** on the Nile at Nuri, in present-day Sudan, after his death.

Assyrians and Persians

In around 665 B.C., a new power appeared. These were the Assyrians *(uh SIHR ee uhnz)* of southwest Asia, who already ruled a large area in the Middle East. The Assyrians conquered the Nubian ruler of Egypt and gained contol of the country, only later to be driven out again by the Babylonians *(bab uh LOH nee uhnz)*. The Babylonians, in turn, were defeated by the Persians in about 525 B.C.

Persia (an ancient land that included parts of what are now Iran and Afghanistan) ruled Egypt for nearly 200 years. The Egyptians had to pay their taxes to the Persian king, and Aramaic *(ar uh MAY ihk)*—a language widely used at this time—became the official language of the government ruling Egypt. Later Persian rulers were very unpopular, especially King Artaxerxes *(ar taks ERKS eez)*, who looted valuable objects and destroyed many buildings. When the Macedonian *(mas uh DOH nee uhn)* emperor Alexander drove the Persians out in 332 B.C., the Egyptians greeted him joyfully.

GREEK AND ROMAN RULE

The Egyptians seem to have welcomed Alexander the Great because he freed them from unpopular Persian rule. But the conquest of Egypt was also a crucial moment in Alexander's career. He took on the role of pharaoh and appeared to show respect for the ancient Egyptian gods.

Alexander founded a new city in the **Delta** region to establish his power. He called it Alexandria, and it became a center of Greek **culture** and learning. Alexander soon left to expand his empire, and he died in 323 B.C. His empire was quickly divided up by his generals.

ALEXANDER THE GREAT (356–323 B.C.)

Alexander was one of the greatest military leaders in history. He became king of Macedon *(mas uh DON)* in northern Greece at the age of 20, when his father was murdered. In 334 B.C., he led his army into Persia to begin an amazing career. He defeated the Persian king, Darius *(duh RY uhs)*, conquered Syria and Babylonia, and then became ruler of Egypt. After this, he extended his empire across Afghanistan and India. His conquests spread Greek influence across the known world.

◀ Greco-Roman **relief** portrait of Alexander the Great, showing him with the symbols of the sun god Amun-Re. Alexander took Egypt from the Persians, who then controlled it, in 332 B.C. After his death in 323 B.C., an essentially Greek dynasty, the Ptolemaic, ruled Egypt until 51 B.C.

The Ptolemies

One of Alexander's generals, called Ptolemy *(TOL uh mee)*, gained control of Egypt and declared himself king. He founded a new **dynasty**, which included many more kings who took the name Ptolemy. This dynasty continued to rule Egypt for another three centuries. During this period, Greek settlers replaced Egyptians in the most powerful positions in government. Alexandria became the capital, famous for its great library and its huge lighthouse—the Pharos *(FAIR ohs)*.

However, the Ptolemies were often at war with neighboring countries, and they found it hard to hold on to their power. In about 67 B.C., an Egyptian army expelled Ptolemy XII from the country. He asked for help from the fast-growing Roman Empire. The Romans sent troops to restore him to the throne.

The Last Queen of Ancient Egypt

Roman influence over Egypt soon grew stronger. In 51 B.C., one of the most famous of all Egypt's rulers took control. Cleopatra VII was determined to regain the lost territories and stay independent of Rome. She and Mark Antony, one of the Roman leaders, became lovers. Their affair led to war with Antony's rivals in Rome, who defeated the Egyptian fleet in 31 B.C. Antony and Cleopatra committed suicide, and the Romans took control of Egypt.

▲ A relief, believed to be a portrait of Queen Cleopatra, dating from the Ptolemaic period. Traces of a grid can be seen, indicating that the relief was either unfinished or was used by sculptors as a model.

THE ANCIENT EGYPTIAN LEGACY

Much of the history and **culture** of the ancient Egyptians was forgotten for many centuries after their empire came to an end. Temples fell out of use, tombs were looted, and stone from the **pyramids** was taken to build other structures. The ability to read **hieroglyphic** script was largely lost.

▼ Howard Carter (kneeling) opens the tomb of Tutankhamun in the Valley of the Kings in 1922.

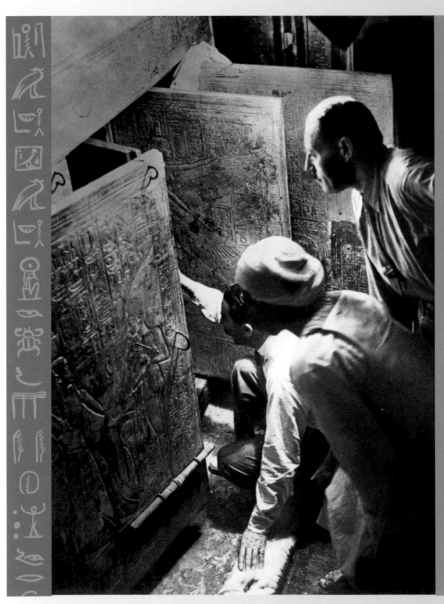

HOWARD CARTER ON DISCOVERING THE TOMB OF KING TUTANKHAMUN

"Slowly, desperately slowly it seemed to us as we watched, the remains of passage debris that encumbered [blocked] the lower part of the doorway were removed.... With trembling hands I made a tiny breach [opening] in the upper left hand corner.... I inserted the candle and peered in, Lord Carnarvon, Lady Evelyn [Lord Carnarvon's daughter] and Callender [an assistant] standing anxiously beside me to hear the verdict.... presently, as my eyes grew accustomed to the light, details of the room within emerged slowly from the mist, strange animals, statues, and gold—everywhere the glint of gold. For the moment—an eternity it must have seemed to the others standing by—I was struck dumb with amazement, and when Lord Carnarvon, unable to stand the suspense any longer, inquired anxiously, 'Can you see anything?' it was all I could do to get out the words, 'Yes, wonderful things.'"

In the 1700's, the material culture of ancient Egypt began to be rediscovered by the West. Architects, artists, and writers became inspired by Egyptian art. An entire branch of history, called Egyptology *(ee jihp TOL uh jee)*, was devised to study ancient Egypt.

The people of Egypt are very proud of their cultural heritage. Many thousands of tourists from all over the world visit Egypt to see the amazing sites of this ancient society.

The Influence of Ancient Egypt

Interest in ancient Egypt and the work done on the **artifacts** found in Egypt have helped to develop the science of **archaeology** and our modern understanding of ancient history. One of the most amazing discoveries in archaeology was made in 1922, when Howard Carter, a British Egyptologist, found the tomb of King Tutankhamun. This tomb had not been opened since ancient times and contained most of its treasures. It is still one of the few tombs of an ancient Egyptian king to have been discovered almost completely intact.

Tutankhamun's four-room tomb contained more than 5,000 objects, including many beautiful carved and gold-covered items. A magnificent, lifelike gold mask of Tutankhamun covered the head and shoulders of the royal **mummy**. The treasures of King Tut, as he is often known, are the most popular museum exhibits in the world. They have traveled far and wide, causing a sensation wherever they are shown.

▲ The mask placed over the face and shoulders of the mummified Tutankhamun is one of the most famous of ancient Egyptian works of art. Crafted from solid gold and inlaid with colored glass and gemstones, the mask was discovered in Tutankhamun's tomb in 1922 by Egyptologist Howard Carter.

GLOSSARY

amulet A charm worn to guard against evil.

archaeologist A scientist who studies the remains of past human **cultures.**

archaeology The scientific study of the remains of past human **cultures.**

artifact An object or the remains of an object, such as a tool, made by people in the past.

artisan A person skilled in some industry or trade.

basalt A hard volcanic rock.

Book of the Dead A collection of texts of prayers, hymns, spells, and other information to guide souls through the afterlife. Egyptians had passages from such texts written on walls inside their tombs or had a copy of a text placed in their tombs.

bronze A metal made mostly of copper and tin.

canopic jar A ceremonial vase used in Egypt, chiefly for holding the entrails (inner parts) of **embalmed** bodies.

cataract Stretches of rocky rapids or waterfalls in a river.

civilization The way of life in a society that features complex economic, governmental, and social systems.

composite Made from two or more different materials.

court The place where a king or emperor lives; also, the family, household, or followers of a king or emperor.

cult A system of religious worship, especially with reference to its ceremonies.

culture A society's arts, beliefs, customs, institutions, inventions, language, technology, and values.

delta A low plain composed of clay, sand, gravel, and other sediments deposited at the mouth of a river.

drought A long period of dry weather.

dynasty A group (usually members of the same family) who rule a place.

ebony A hard, black wood found in tropical and semitropical regions of the world.

embalm To treat a dead body with spices, chemicals, or drugs to keep it from decaying.

excavate To uncover or unearth by digging, especially used of archaeological sites.

fertile Able to easily produce crops (when used about land or soil).

flail A hand tool used to separate out the seeds from such grain crops as wheat.

flint A hard stone which gives a sharp edge when split.

flood plain A low-lying region of land next to a river made of soil deposited by floods.

hereditary Offices or privileges that are passed down from parents or ancestors.

hieroglyphics A form of writing in which picture symbols represent ideas and sounds.

ivory A hard substance that makes up the main part of the tusks and teeth of certain animals. The tusks of the African elephant are the major source of ivory.

legend A folk story, often set in the past, which may be based in truth, but which may also contain fictional or fantastic elements. Legends are similar to myths, but myths often are about such sacred topics as gods.

mortuary Concerning death, burial, or mourning.

mortuary temple The place where the **cult** of a dead ruler was celebrated and remembered.

mummification The process of making a **mummy.**

mummy A dead body that has been preserved and that still has some of its soft tissue—that is, a body that has decayed only to a limited degree. The preservation of the body may have been done using artificial means, such as salts and resins. Or, the preservation may have been natural—for example, a body left in a dry, cold climate was sometimes naturally preserved.

natron A powdery mineral consisting of sodium carbonate and salt, used at times to draw the moisture from corpses before the process of **mummification.**

nemes A striped cloth headdress worn by the pharaohs. The nemes hung down on both sides of the face and was gathered at the back in something similar to a ponytail.

noble or **nobleman** or **-woman** A person of high standing in his or her **culture.**

nomarch A local official who ruled a district or province.

nomes Provinces into which ancient Egypt was divided.

ore A mixture of minerals found naturally, from which a valuable mineral (such as copper) may be extracted.

papyrus A tall plant that grows in water or very wet soil. Also the material for writing on that was made from fibers of the papyrus plant by the ancient Egyptians, Greeks, and Romans.

pyramid A large building or other structure with a square base and four smooth, triangular-shaped sides that come to a point at the top.

quarry A place where stone is dug out for use in building.

reliefs Sculptures in which figures or designs project from their background.

ritual A solemn or important act or ceremony, often religious in nature.

sanctuary In an Egyptian temple, the most sacred area of that temple, where images of a god or goddess were kept.

sarcophagus A stone coffin, sometimes made to contain a smaller wooden coffin.

scribe A person whose occupation is writing, especially copying manuscripts.

silt Very fine particles of earth, sand, clay, or similar matter, carried by moving water.

sphinx An imaginary creature of ancient myths. According to various tales, the sphinx had the body of a lion and the head of a human, falcon, or ram. Some sphinxes also had wings and a serpent tail.

stele An upright slab or pillar of stone with writing, a sculptured design, or the like (plural, stelae).

sun disk A round, flat gold disk which represents the sun.

torso The body of a human or statue, not including the head, arms, or legs.

turquoise A mineral widely used as a gemstone; turquoise ranges in color from sky-blue to blue-green or yellow-green.

vizier The pharaoh's chief minister and official, who oversaw the daily running of the government.

ADDITIONAL RESOURCES

Books

Ancient Egypt
by Geraldine Harris (Chelsea House, 2007)

Ancient Egypt
by George Hart (DK Publishing, 2004)

Everyday Life in Ancient Egypt
by Nathaniel Harris (Sea to Sea
Publications, 2006)

*Great Ancient Egypt Projects You Can
Build Yourself*
 by Carmella Van Vleet (Nomad Press, 2006)

If I Were a Kid in Ancient Egypt
edited by Lou Waryncia and Kenneth M. Sheldon
(Cricket Books, 2006)

*The Mummy: Unwrap the Ancient Secrets of the
Mummies' Tombs*
by Joyce A. Tyldesley (Barnes & Noble
Books, 2002)

Pyramid by David Macaulay (Houghton Mifflin,
1975)

Voices of Ancient Egypt
by Kay Winters (National Geographic, 2003)

Web Sites

http://www.ancientegypt.co.uk/

http://www.ancienthistory.about.com/od/egypt/Ancient_Egypt.htm

http://www.bbc.co.uk/history/ancient/egyptians/

http://www.egyptianmyths.net/

http://www.guardians.net/egypt/kids/index.htm

http://www.mnsu.edu/emuseum/prehistory/egypt/index.shtml

http://www.nationalgeographic.co.uk/pyramids/pyramids.html

http://www.sis.gov.eg/En/History

http://www.touregypt.net/egyptantiquities

INDEX

Acknowledgments

The Art Archive: 1 (Egyptian Museum, Cairo/Alfredo Dagli Orti), 5 (Gianni Dagli Orti), 10 (Egyptian Museum, Cairo/Alfredo Dagli Orti), 16 (Gianni Dagli Orti), 17 (Egyptian Museum, Cairo/Gianni Dagli Orti), 18 (Musée du Louvre, Paris/Gianni Dagli Orti), 20 (Egyptian Museum, Cairo/Gianni Dagli Orti), 23 (Egyptian Museum, Cairo/Alfredo Dagli Orti), 24, 27 (Gianni Dagli Orti), 32 (Gianni Dagli Orti), 37 (Gianni Dagli Orti), 41 (Gianni Dagli Orti), 42 (Musée du Louvre, Paris/Gianni Dagli Orti), 43 (Musée du Louvre, Paris/Gianni Dagli Orti), 49 (Musée du Louvre, Paris/Gianni Dagli Orti), 51 (Bibliothèque Musée du Louvre, Paris/Gianni Dagli Orti), 55; **Bridgeman Art Library**: 39b (British Museum, London); **Corbis**: 7 (Alinari Archives), 13 (Free Agents Limited/Dallas and John Heaton), 36 (Michael Nicholson), 58 (Hulton-Deutsch Collection); **iStockphoto**: 34, 35 (Karim Hesham); **Shutterstock**: 4 (Holger Mette), 6 (Styve Reineck); **Werner Forman Archive**: 8 (Egyptian Museum, Cairo), 9 (British Museum, London), 12, 14 (Egyptian Museum, Cairo), 15 (Egyptian Museum, Berlin), 19 (Egyptian Museum, Cairo), 21 (Egyptian Museum, Cairo), 22 (E. Strouhal), 26 (Egyptian Museum, Cairo), 28 (Fitzwilliam Museum, Cambridge), 29 (E. Strouhal, Egyptian Museum, Turin), 30 (Egyptian Museum, Cairo), 31 (E. Strouhal, Naprstek Museum, Prague), 33, 38 (Musée du Louvre, Paris), 39 (Musées Royaux du Cinquantenaire, Brussels), 40 (Egyptian Museum, Cairo), 44 (British Museum, London), 45 (University College London, Petrie Museum), 46 (Egyptian Museum, Turin), 47 (British Museum, London), 48 (E. Strouhal), 50 (E. Strouhal), 52 (British Museum, London), 53 (E. Strouhal), 54 (Egyptian Museum, Cairo), 56 (Musées Royaux du Cinquantenaire, Brussels), 57 (Schindler Collection, New York), 59 (Egyptian Museum, Cairo).

Cover image: **Shutterstock** (Miroslav Tomasovic)
Back cover image: **Shutterstock** (Joop Snijder, Jr.)